Then breeze turns to gale,
with a whistle and roar!

MARIA CORRIGAN AND KELLY BRODIE

ILLUSTRATED BY JULIE MELLAN

TIZZY THROWS A FIZZY

ISBN: 979-8-9852121-3-6

Printed in the United States of America.

Thank you to our editor, Brooke Vitale.

Tizzy the turtle is ready to play.
His big blue kite's perfect for
this sunny day.

He lifts his kite high, and
the wind makes it soar . . .

The kite swirls and twirls,
as it wraps 'round a tree.
Tizzy pulls hard, but he
can't get it free!

His kite's clearly tangled, it seems to be stuck.
Perhaps a big leap and a swing will bring luck.

Grasping the string, he spins quickly around.
Now Tizzy feels dizzy and falls to the ground!

Feelings of panic deep down start to grow,
But Tizzy won't stop, up the tree he must go!

So, grabbing the tree trunk, he reaches up high,
But Tizzy's too weak, and he soon starts to cry!

He's tried and he's tried, but his kite won't come down.
Now Tizzy's mad, and he's starting to frown.

He jumps up and down, and he stomps side to side.
His shell is too small for his feelings to hide!

As tears roll down his cheek, he hears someone say,
"There's no need to worry, friend. You'll be okay."

Sydney the Sloth says, "Now Tizzy, don't pout!
Just take a deep breath in, then let that breath out."

"We'll do it together, count in 1, 2, 3.

1...
2...
3...

Then breathe out your worries
and stay calm with me."

Feeling much better, Tizzy has a plan,
He spots a big rock and he knows
that he can!

He nudges the rock, as his
friends gather near.
With a rumble, it tumbles,
then all start to cheer.

The rock lands just right
and with all Tizzy's might,
He climbs up on top,
setting free his blue kite.

THUMP!

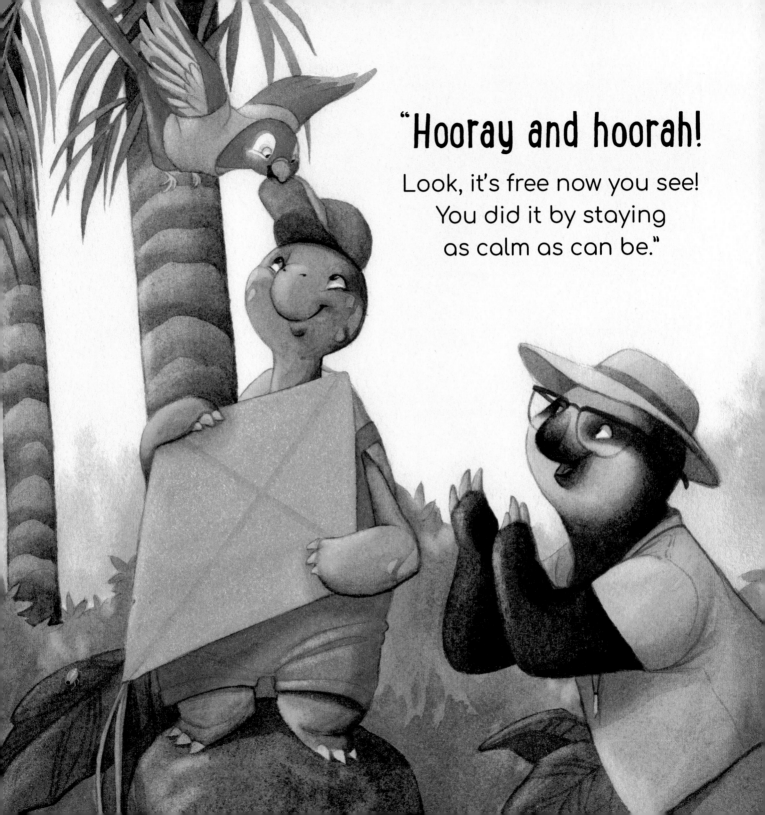

"Hooray and hoorah!
Look, it's free now you see!
You did it by staying
as calm as can be."

With a smile ear to ear, Tizzy's joy filled the air.
You're never alone when you're with friends who care.

60389949R00015